Poems about Feelings

Selected by
Amanda Earl & Danielle Sensier

Illustrated by
Frances Lloyd

Wayland

Titles in the series
Poems about . . .

Animals	**Food**
Colours	**Journeys**
Feelings	**Weather**

For Chloë, Jonjo and Joshua.

Series editor: Catherine Baxter
Designer: Loraine Hayes

First published in 1994 by
Wayland (Publishers) Ltd
61 Western Road, Hove
East Sussex BN3 1JD, England

British Library Cataloguing in Publication Data

Earl, Amanda
   Feelings. – (Poems About . . . Series)
   I. Title II. Sensier, Danielle
   III. Series
   808.819353

ISBN 0 7502 0972 0

Front cover Three happy girls/design S. Balley.

Typeset by Dorchester Typesetting
Group Ltd., Dorset, England.
Printed and bound in Italy by
G. Canale & C.S.p.A., Turin.

Poets' nationalities

Kit Wright	English
Cheryl	English
A. A. Milne	English
John Agard	(British/Guyanese)
Roger McGough	English
Jeff Moss	American
Teresita Fernandez	Cuban
Kassia	Greek
Mihri Hatun	Turkish
Richard Edwards	English
Alethia Walker	English
Marchette Chute	Canadian
Kit Wright	English
Langston Hughes	American
John Foster	Scottish
Nga Bach Thi Tran	Asian

Contents

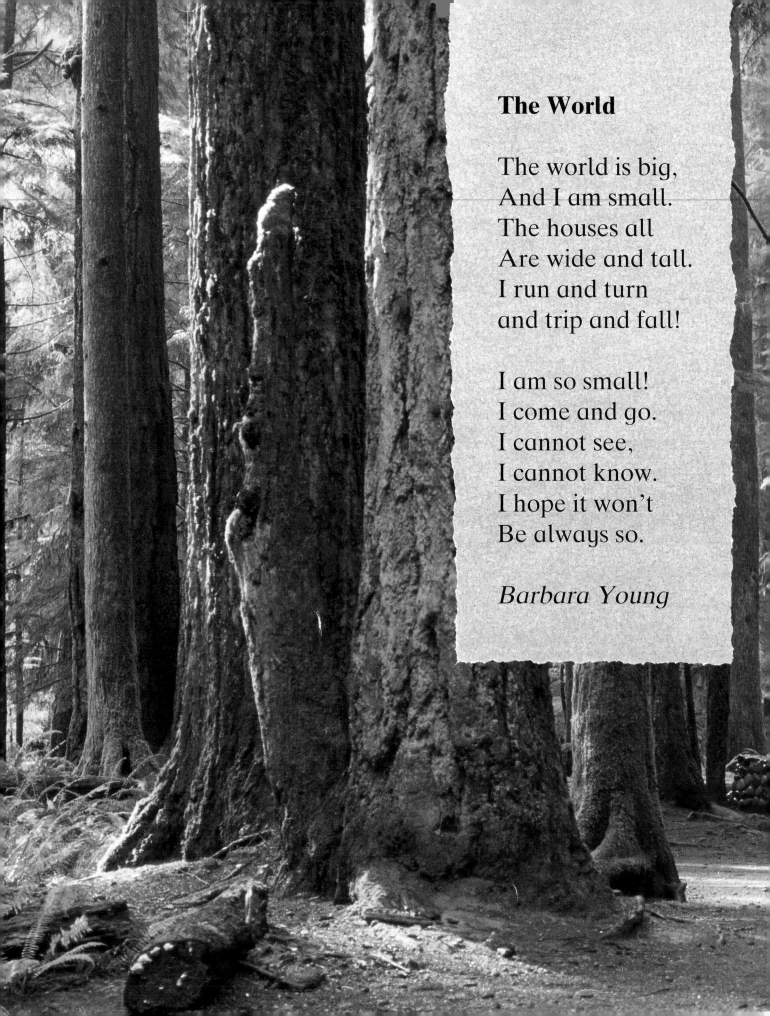

The World

The world is big,
And I am small.
The houses all
Are wide and tall.
I run and turn
and trip and fall!

I am so small!
I come and go.
I cannot see,
I cannot know.
I hope it won't
Be always so.

Barbara Young

How I see it

Some say the world's
A hopeless case:
A speck of dust
In all that space.
It's certainly
A scruffy place.
Just one hope
For the human race
That I can see;
Me. I'm
ACE!

Kit Wright

My Life

I'm Cheryl the Peril, I'm proud to relate
I know what I like
and
I know what I hate.
I hate rainy days and wet afternoons
I hate cars and yellow balloons
I like making friends and the buzz of a bee
HEY, I like being ME!

Cheryl
(child poet)

Happiness

John had
Great big
Waterproof
Boots on;
John had a
Great Big
Waterproof
Hat;
John had a
Great Big
Waterproof
Mackintosh –
And that
(said John)
   Is
   That.

A. A. Milne

Where does Laughter Begin?

Does it start in your head
and spread to your toes?

Does it start in your cheeks
and grow downwards so
till your knees feel weak?

Does it start with a tickle
in your tummy so
till you want to jump right out

of your skin?
Or does laughter simply begin

with your mouth?

John Agard

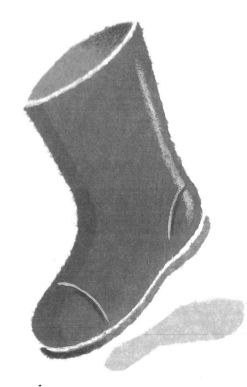

8

Scowling

When I see you
scowling

I want to turn you
upside down

and see you smile!

Roger McGough

Bad Mood Day

Keep away
It's a bad mood day,
I could make a noise,
Break my toys.
I could be very bad,
Make mum sad.
I could smash a mug
Spill the milk jug
It's a bad mood day.
A bad bad day.

Class poem by 5-6 year olds

11

I'm Going to Say I'm Sorry

I'm going to say I'm sorry.
It's time for this quarrel to end.
I know that we both didn't mean it
And each of us misses a friend.
It isn't much fun being angry
And arguing's just the worst,
So I'm going to say I'm sorry . . .
Just as soon as you say sorry first!

Jeff Moss

Courage

Courage is when you're
allergic to cats and

your new friend says can
you come to her house to
play after school and

stay to dinner then
maybe go skating and
sleep overnight? And,

she adds, you can pet
her small kittens! Oh,
how you ache to. It

takes courage to
say 'no' to all that.

Emily Hearn

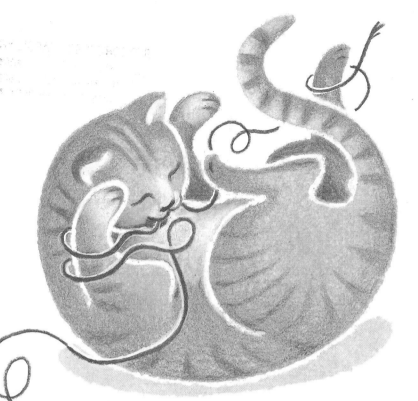

From **Ugly Things** (a song)

If you put a bit of love
into ugly things
you'll see that your sadness
will begin to change colour.

Teresita Fernandez

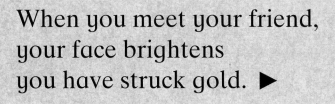

When you meet your friend,
your face brightens
you have struck gold. ▶

Kassia
(translated by P. Diehl)

At one glance
I loved you
with a thousand hearts.

Mihri Hatun
(translated by Talat S. Halman)

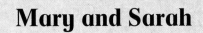

Mary and Sarah

Mary likes smooth things,
Things that glide:
Sleek skis swishing down a mountainside.

    Sarah likes rough things,
    Things that snatch:
    Boats with barnacled bottoms, thatch.

Mary likes smooth things,
Things all mellow:
Milk, silk, runny honey, tunes on a cello.

    Sarah likes rough things,
    Things all troubly:
    Crags, snags, bristles, thistles, fields left stubbly.

Mary says – polish,
Sarah says – rust,
Mary says – mayonnaise,
Sarah says – crust.

Sarah says – hedgehogs,
Mary says – seals,
Sarah says – sticklebacks,
Mary says – eels.

Give me, says Mary
The slide of a stream,
The touch of a petal,
A bowl of ice-cream.

Give me, says Sarah,
The gales of a coast,
The husk of a chestnut,
A plate of burnt toast . . .

Mary and Sarah –
They'll never agree
Till peaches and coconuts
Grow on one tree.

Richard Edwards

17

No Friends

I have got no friends –
I can't ask anyone if they
Will lend me felt-tip pens.
There is a girl across the
Table who has got a horse
And stable,
I know all these things
Because I hear her talking.
I am all alone on my table.

Every day when I watch them play,
I don't understand what they say,
They won't let me join in,
I stay in locked away,
My mum and dad say go out,
It is a nice day,
But if I haven't got
Any friends

     I can't.

Alethia Walker
(aged 10)

My Teddy Bear

A teddy bear is a faithful friend.
You can pick him up at either end.
His fur is the colour of breakfast toast,
And he's always there when you need him most.

Marchette Chute

Grandad

Grandad's dead
Am I'm sorry about that.

He'd a huge black overcoat.
He felt proud in it.
You could have hidden
A football crowd in it.
Far too big –
It was a lousy fit
But Grandad didn't
Mind a bit.
He wore it all winter
With a squashed black hat.

Now he's dead
And I'm sorry about that.

He'd got twelve stories.
I'd heard every one of them
Hundreds of times
But that was the fun of them:
You knew what was coming
So you could join in.
He'd got big hands
And brown, grooved skin
And when he laughed
It knocked you flat.

Now he's dead
Am I'm sorry about that.

Kit Wright

Hope

Sometimes when I'm lonely,
Don't know why,
Keep thinkin' I won't be lonely
By and by.

Langston Hughes

A Saying from Zimbabwe

If you can walk
You can dance
If you can talk
You can sing

Traditional

25

First Day at School

My first day at school today.
Funny sort of day.
Didn't seem to learn much.
Seemed all we did was play.
Then teacher wrote some letters
On a board all painted black,
And then we had a story and . . .
I don't think I'll go back.

Rod Hull

Four O'Clock Friday

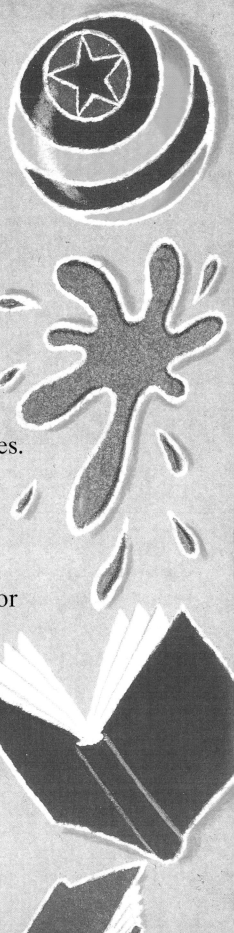

Four o'clock, Friday, I'm home at last.
Time to forget the week that has passed.

On Monday, at break, they stole my ball
And threw it over the playground wall.

On Tuesday morning, I came in late,
But they were waiting behind the gate.

On Wednesday afternoon, in games
They threw mud at me and called me names.

Yesterday, they laughed after the test
'Cause my marks were lower than the rest.

Today, they trampled my books on the floor
And I was kept in, because I swore.

Four o'clock, Friday, at last I'm free.
For two whole days they can't get at me.

John Foster

From **Dream of a Bird**

You ask me, what did I dream?
I dreamt I became a bird.
You ask me, why did I want to become a bird?
I really wanted to have wings.
You ask me, why did I want wings?
These wings would help me fly back to my country.
You ask me, why did I want to go back there?
Because I wanted to find something I missed.
You ask me, what do I miss?
I miss the place where I lived as a child.
You ask me, what was that place like?
That place was happy, my family was close together.

Nga Bach Thi Tran

How to use this book

Poetry is a very enjoyable area of literature and children take to it naturally, usually beginning with nursery rhymes. It's what happens next that can make all the difference! This series of thematic poetry anthologies keeps poetry alive and enjoyable for young children.

When using these books there are several ways in which you can help a child to enjoy poetry and to understand the ways in which words can be carefully chosen and sculpted to convey different atmospheres and meanings. Try to encourage the following:

- Joining in when the poem is read out loud.
- Talking about favourite words, phrases or images.
- Discussing the illustration and photographs.
- Miming facial expressions to suit the mood of the poems.
- Acting out events in the poems.
- Copying out the words.
- Learning favourite poems by heart.
- Discussing the difference between a poem and a story.
- Clapping hands to rhythmic poems.
- Talking about metaphors/similes eg what kind of weather would a lion be? What colour would sadness be? What would it taste like? If you could hold it, how would it feel?

It is inevitable that, at some point, children will want to write poems themselves. Writing a poem is, however, only one way of enjoying poetry. With the above activities, children can be encouraged to appreciate and delight in this unique form of communication.

Picture acknowledgements

Ace 4-5 (Laszlo Willinger), 13 (Gabe Palmer); Cephas 10 (Peter O'Neil); Collections/Anthea Sieveking 18, 21; Sally & Richard Greenhill 7; Eye Ubiquitous 29 (Roger Chester); Life File 23 (John Cox), 24 (Nicola Sutton), 26 (Nicola Sutton); Trevor Wood 9; Tony Stone Worldwide cover, 6 (Chip Henderson), 15 (Don Smetzer); Julia Waterlow 12.

Text acknowledgements

For permission to reprint copyright material the publishers gratefully acknowledge the following: Barbara Young for 'The World', from Christopher O!, © 1947 and renewed 1975 by Barbara Young, by permission of David McKay Co., a division of Random House, Inc.; Kit Wright for 'How I See It' and 'Grandad'; Reed Book Services for 'Happiness' by A. A. Milne; John Agard c/o Caraline Sheldon Literary Agency for 'Where Does Laughter Begin', from Laughter Is An Egg published by Viking 1990; Roger McGough for 'Scowling' from Pillow Talk, reprinted by permission of the Peters, Fraser & Dunlop Group Ltd; 'From Ugly Things' by Teresita Fernández, translated by Margaret Randall; Mihri Hatun for 'At One Glance', reprinted by permission of Talat S. Halman; Richard Edwards for 'Mary and Sarah' from A Mouse In My Roof, first published by Orchard Books. © 1988 Orchard Books; Marchette Chute for 'My Teddy Bear' from Rhymes About Us by Marchette Chute. Published 1974 by E. P. Dutton. Copyright © 1974 Marchette. Reprinted by permission of Elizabeth Roach; David Higham Associates for 'Hope' and 'A Saying From Zimbabwe' by Langston Hughes; Hodder & Stoughton Limited for 'First Day of School' from The Reluctant Poet by Rod Hull; John Foster for 'Four O'Clock Friday', first published in A Fifth Poetry Book (Oxford University Press), included by permission of the author; Martin International PTY Ltd for 'Dream of a Bird' by Nga Bach Thi Tran. While every effort has been made to secure permission, in some cases it has proved impossible to trace the copyright holders.

Index of first lines